너와의 걸음걸이
Walking with you
4

정송전 한영시집

Korean-English Poems Collection of Jeong Song Jeon

을지출판공사

■ 자서自序

　삶의 다양한 모습과 고단한 숨결이 시의 눈을 틔우고 오만 가지 허드레 잡념까지도 내게로 와서 시가 되었을 때, 그것은 돌올한 내 시의 성취라면 성취라고 감히 자부한다.
　나는 내 시집 〈내 이렇게 살다가〉의 자서에 다음과 같이 적은 적이 있다.
　'나의 여정은 분명 저녁나절쯤이지만 나의 시는 아직 새벽이다. 그래서 하염없이 회안에 젖는다.'
　내 삶이 어느 날 느닷없이 내가 아닌 것처럼 비춰지기도 했으며 삶의 질곡이 부질없이 그리움으로 다가오기도 했음을 고백한다. 그러나 그럴 때마다 내 삶의 심지를 곧추세우는 의연한 '여유'가 나를 건져 내기도 했다. 이것이 내 시의 이력이자 본령이라는 것을 나는 잊지 않는다.
　끝으로, 이 영문시집 펴내는데 있어 아내(신미자)와 아들(정주헌) 노고가 컸음을 밝혀 둔다.

　　　　　　　　2022. 5. 10

　　　　　　　　　　　지은이 정송전

■ The Preface of the Poet

When the various aspects and the weary breath of life put forth a bud of poetry and even tens of thousands of miscellaneous trivia thoughts come to me and become poetry, if I can call it, I dare to say that's the accomplishment of my outstanding poetry.

I once wrote the following in my essay for my collection of poems, 〈Living like this〉.

'My journey is certainly about the evening, but my poem is still dawn. So, I get soaked in endless remorse.'

I confess that one day my life suddenly felt like it wasn't me, and that life's ordeal came to me in vain longing. But every time that happened, the resolute 'Composure' that made my life upright, saved me. I do not forget that this is the history and the original characteristic of my poetry.

To conclude, I would like to acknowledge the efforts of my wife (Mija Shin) and son (Jooheon Jeong) in writing this English poem collection.

2022. 5. 10

Author Jeong Song jeon

차례

- 자서自序 The Preface of the Poet · 2
- 저자 약력 · 164

제1부 삶의 위무와 격려의 울타리로서
Part 1 As a fence of comfort and encouragement in life

굿판 Performing an exorcism / 10
섬사람 · 3 Islander · 3 / 14
내 다시 소년이 되었지 I become a boy again / 16
풍속도 A cultural landscape / 18
교외에서 In the suburb / 22
관사에서 In the official residence / 24
그 시대 That era / 26
이별 뒤 After a farewell / 30
여름날 그때 그곳에 On a summer day there / 32
피끝 냇가 A stream in the Pikkeut village / 34
소박데기 A deserted wife / 38
대부도 여신女神 The goddess of Daebu Island / 40
탈속脫俗 Unworldliness / 42
다시, 출발점에서 Again, at the starting point / 44
바람은 The wind is / 46

──────────────────── Table of ontents

제2부 그리움은 숨어 살고 기다림은 울며 산다
Part 2   Longing lives in hiding and waiting lives in crying

사랑할 때 When in love / 50
빛의 숨결 The breath of light / 52
바닷가 아침에 By the sea in the morning / 54
바람의 침묵·1 The silence of the wind·1 / 56
바람의 침묵·2 The silence of the wind·2 / 58
바른 말 An outspoken right word / 60
박꽃바람 The gourd flower wind / 62
독도에게 To Dokdo Island / 64
바람 속에서 In the wind / 68
안 부·1 Best Regards·1 / 70
침 묵 Silence / 74
어느 서해안 선에서 At one west coastline / 76
백문서원 Baekmun traditional auditorium / 78
귀 향 Returning home / 80
세월 아득히 Afar the years / 82
그리움 일랴 The longing is / 84

차례

제3부 이별의 뒤란에서 해후의 뜨락으로
Part 3 From the back of farewell to the garden of a meeting

바람 속으로 Into the winds / 88

백 자 A white porcelain / 90

흘러가는 구름을 바라보며 Looking at the flowing clouds / 92

물속에서 흔들린다 Sways in the water / 94

빛의 울림을 그린다 I draw the echoes of light / 96

어느 날 One day / 98

너와의 걸음걸이 Walking with you / 100

폐교 운동장 The playground of a closed school / 104

종소리와 비천상 The sound of a bell and the image of a flying fairy / 106

어느 이국 하늘 아래서도 Under a foreign sky also / 108

바람의 말 · 2 The words of the wind · 2 / 110

소용돌이 속에서 In the whirlpool / 112

꽃과 삶 Flowers and life / 114

어떤 기다림 A certain wait / 118

연꽃 소묘 The sketch of a lotus / 120

봄 흙으로 젖어 계세요 Please stay wet with spring soil / 122

Table of ontents

제4부 보내고 나면 돌아오는 것들
Part 4 Things that come back after sending

하늘 아래서 Under the sky / 128

겨울나무 · 2 A winter tree · 2 / 130

호수와 달과 산 The lake, the moon, and the mountain / 132

어떤 풍경화 Some landscape painting / 134

이순 앞에서 Before the age of sixty / 136

아무렇지도 않게 꽃은 피어나 Flowers bloom indifferently / 138

마음 어디에 · 1 Somewhere in my mind · 1 / 140

마음 어디에 · 2 Somewhere in my mind · 2 / 142

마음 어디에 · 3 Somewhere in my mind · 3 / 144

모습 그 여운으로 A shape, with that lingering imagery / 146

비어 있는 음향 Empty sound / 150

설해목 The broken tree by heavy snow / 154

꽃씨 A flower seed / 156

봄은 정녕 자네의 눈빛일세 The spring is truly your eyes / 160

한 그루 나무로 서서 Standing as a tree / 162

제1부 Part 1

삶의 위무와 격려의 울타리로서
As a fence of comfort and encouragement in life

내 또래의 슬픔을 안다
내 또래의 그리움을 안다.

춘궁기가 무섭던
내 소년은
속절도 없이 가버렸지만

내 또래의 하늘을 안다
내 또래의 사랑을 안다.
- 「그 시대」 중에서

I know the sorrow of my age
I know the longing of my age.

Afraid of the spring austerity
My boy
Had gone away helplessly, but

I know the sky of my age
I know the love of my age.
- The part of 「That era」

굿판

징소리는 고단한 목소리로
헤매는 구름을 부른다.
한밤중 한恨을 풀어 날리는
지친 징소리
은은하고 보드랍던 이승의 여운과
영혼이 진동하는 저승의 고개 숙인 얼굴로
사는 것 같지 않게 허공에 떠돌더라도
아무것도 엿보지 말고 잠들어라.
어떻게 살다가 어떻게 가는지
범람하는 어둠과 더불어
가느다랗게 촛불에 흐른다.
이 굿판 속 무당은
바리데기 좌편에 앉은 탱화 앞에서
거룩하고 장한 효성 탐복하고 눈물질까
한밤중의 징소리를 멈춰라.
귓가에 부서지는 네 영혼의 절규는
허공에 퍼져
햇빛도 소낙비도 모두 씻어버리는
그런 목소리이어늘
징그럽던 허물을 벗기는 아픔일러나.

Performing an exorcism

The sound of a gong calls the wandering clouds
By a tired voice.
Releasing and flying regrets at midnight,
That exhausted sound of the gong
The delicate and soft lingering imagery of this life and
The drooping face of the afterlife where the soul vibrates,
Even if it is roaming in the air unlike living the world,
Sleep without peeping at anything.
How to live and how to leave
Along with the flooding darkness
It flows thinly into the candlelight.
The shaman of this performing an exorcism
Does she shed tears with admiration to that great and praiseworthy filial piety
In front of the altar portrait of Buddha sitting on the left side of *Baridegi?
Stop the sound of the gong at midnight.
The scream your soul that breaks near my ear
Spreading in the air and
Washing away all the sunshine and sudden showers

자지러지는 낱낱의 사람들에게
이제는 녹슨 놋쇠로 다가와
산 자를 위한 여운으로 메아리쳐 다오.
세상사를 승화시켜
영롱한 햇살 아래
내가 네가 되게.

It's such a voice,

It might be an ache of taking off the creepy skin.

To every single person of chattering

Please approach as rusty brass now and

Echo as lingering imagery for the living.

Sublimating the worldly work

Under the brilliant sunlight

To make me be you.

* Baridegi is a young goddess, played in a shamanic ritual that comforts the souls of the dead and leads them to the underworld. It is mythical filial piety who endures all kinds of hardships, sacrifices herself, and seeks immortal medicine to heal her parents.

섬사람 · 3

용광로에서 치솟은 태양은
하늘의 사연도 모른 채
구름과 바람과 향기를 들깨운다.

꽃이 어우러진 마당으로
아침은 나와 앉는다
이슬을 그렁그렁 달고
고요 속으로 여운이 흐른다
하늘은 풀잎처럼 바람에 눕는다.

뱃고동 소리로
물때를 알아 섬, 섬, 섬
달빛에 부서지는 파도를 낚는다.

너는 나에게
싱그러운 젊음을 경작케 해 다오.

짠기 밴 덧니를 보여 다오
우리는 모두 바다가 되자
썰물 됐다 밀물 됐다 하는.

Islander · 3

The sun soaring from the furnace
Unknowing the story of the sky
Wakes up clouds, winds, and fragrance by shaking.

Into the yard where flowers bloom
The morning comes out and sit
Wearing dew waterily
The lingering feeling flows to the silence
The sky lies down in the winds like a grass leaf.

With the sound of the boat horn
Knowing the tide time, island, island, island
Catching the waves crashing by moonlight.

You allow me
To cultivate fresh youth.

Show me your salty projecting tooth
Let's all become the sea
Being the ebb and flow of the tide.

내 다시 소년이 되었지

하늘을 풀어 놓은 광장에서
돌에 눌린 노란 싹을 보았지.

잎새 사이로 내뵈는 햇볕을 쬐어
눈 뜨는 소망을 보았지.

광장에서
달콤한 언어들이
숱한 꿈을 조각하는데

하늘도 땅도
보이지 않는 세계로 미끄러지며
내 다시 소년이 되었지.

I become a boy again

In the square that released the sky
I saw the yellow sprout pressed against the stone.

Exposed to the sunshine which is appearing among leaves
I saw the wish that opened eyes.

In the square
Sweet languages
Were sculpting plentiful dreams

The sky and the earth also
Was sliding into the invisible world,
I became a boy again.

풍속도

봄을 타는 누우런 장막 속으로
버리고 온 사랑채 문고리가
밤새 덜렁거리고
인정 한 올 풀어
젖은 까치발에 휘감고
들녘 바람에 날려 간 시름.

봄비도 다녀가고
초록 다홍 예사로움 속에
지금 나는
어디에 있는가.

장독대 비슷이
그늘 드릴 살구꽃이
하마 피었으련만

가기 싫어,
주저앉던 간밤의 꿈길.

A cultural landscape

Into the yellowish curtain which gets spring fever
The doorknob of the guest house that had been thrown away
Has rattled all night
Unwinding a strand of warm mind
Wrapping it on its wet tiptoe,
The anxiety had blown away by the field wind.

The spring rain also had come by and
Inside the usuality of green and scarlet
Now
Where am I?

Obliquely at the platform for crocks
Apricot blossoms which will shade
Almost will bloom, but

Not want to go,
The dream of last night, which had flopped down.

그래도 먼동은 오는가
히뜩이는 햇빛은 알 리 없겠지.

겨울나무는 맨몸으로
눈을 뜨고
종이에 싸 둔
꽃, 씨앗들은 눈망울 굴리며
어떤 하늘을 열고 있을까.

초록빛 크레용으로 산과 들
푸렁 콩밭과 바람을 그린다.

Is the dawning sky still coming?
The sparkling sunlight might not know it.

The winter tree with bare body
Opens its eyes
And wrapped with paper,
Those flowers and seeds are rolling their eyes
What kind of sky are they opening?

With a green crayon, I draw the mountain and the field,
The greenish bean field, and the wind.

교외에서

나를 떠밀던 표정들이
바람 없는 공간에 발을 모두고 서서
나를 날린다.

앙금 같은 계절에
젖은 하늘이 다가와
나를 날린다.

고단한 언어들은
성내던 모습으로
잠이 들었다.

늘 잠겨 있는 방문 앞에서
나는
부활의 숨결로 어지럽다.

내 모든 것이
동화가 된다
무지개가 뜬 하늘 가까이
손때 묻은
나의 시선에 내가 가득하다.

In the suburb

The look that has pushed me
Stands with feet close together in a windless space
Blows me away.

In the season like sediment
The wet sky approaches
Blows me away.

The tired languages
Have fallen asleep
With an angry look.

In front of a room door that is always locked
I am
Dizzy with the breath of resurrection.

All about myself
Are assimilated
Near the sky with a rainbow
In my gaze of stained hands
There are full of me.

관사에서

빈 관사의 황톳길을 오르다가 미끄러져도
환상 속 그대 우산으로
아무렇지가 않소.

벽지에 풀칠을 해 놓고
일손이 잡히지 않아
눈을 꼬옥 감고
며칠을 지내고 있소
곰팡이 냄새도 익숙해졌소.

모두가 다 옹색하기만 한 일상
이상해요,
노을로 물들이는 것은
왠지 신기하기만 하오.

혼자 사는 사람이 되어
밤은 밤으로 태어나고
나는 그 속에 안주하오.

In the official residence

Even if I slide down while climbing to the red clay
road in the official residence
Due to your umbrella in the fantasy
I am safe.

After pasting glue on the wallpaper
Couldn't focus on working
With closing my eyes tight
I've been spending several days,
Have been used to the smell of fungus.

The daily life when everyone is poor
It's weird,
To color with the sunset,
It's just amazing for some reason.

Being a person who lives alone
Night is born as the night and
I am settled into that inside.

그 시대

내 또래의 슬픔을 안다
내 또래의 그리움을 안다.

춘궁기가 무섭던
내 소년은
속절도 없이 가버렸지만

내 또래의 하늘을 안다
내 또래의 사랑을 안다.

먹구름에 가려진 무지개로
뭔가 이 세상에 있는가 보다
그 때부터 느끼고 살아왔지만

내 또래의 아쉬움을 준다
내 또래의 부끄러움을 준다.

밑지고 살아온
내 소년이
이승의 원가原價를 꿈이라지만

That era

I know the sorrow of my age
I know the longing of my age.

Afraid of the spring austerity
My boy
Had gone away helplessly, but

I know the sky of my age
I know the love of my age.

With the rainbow hidden by black clouds
There must be something in this world
Although I have felt it and lived since then

It gives me the inconvenience of my age
It gives me the shame of my age.

My boy, who has lived of losing out
Calls the cost of this life
A dream, though

내 또래의 고통을 알기 때문이다
내 또래의 세상을 알기 때문이다.

In the official residence

Even if I slide down while climbing to the red clay road in the official residence
Due to your umbrella in the fantasy
I am safe.

After pasting glue on the wallpaper
Couldn't focus on working
With closing my eyes tight
I've been spending several days,
Have been used to the smell of fungus.

The daily life when everyone is poor
It's weird,
To color with the sunset,
It's just amazing for some reason.

Being a person who lives alone
Night is born as the night and
I am settled into that inside.

그 시대

내 또래의 슬픔을 안다
내 또래의 그리움을 안다.

춘궁기가 무섭던
내 소년은
속절도 없이 가버렸지만

내 또래의 하늘을 안다
내 또래의 사랑을 안다.

먹구름에 가려진 무지개로
뭔가 이 세상에 있는가 보다
그 때부터 느끼고 살아왔지만

내 또래의 아쉬움을 준다
내 또래의 부끄러움을 준다.

밑지고 살아온
내 소년이
이승의 원가原價를 꿈이라지만

That era

I know the sorrow of my age
I know the longing of my age.

Afraid of the spring austerity
My boy
Had gone away helplessly, but

I know the sky of my age
I know the love of my age.

With the rainbow hidden by black clouds
There must be something in this world
Although I have felt it and lived since then

It gives me the inconvenience of my age
It gives me the shame of my age.

My boy, who has lived of losing out
Calls the cost of this life
A dream, though

내 또래의 고통을 알기 때문이다
내 또래의 세상을 알기 때문이다.

Because I know the agony of my age
Because I know the world of my age.

이별 뒤

이제 와서 새로이
손 내밀어 건네준
산과 들의 풍경.

이야기는 모두 포장해 둔 채
그을린 시간을 헤아려본다.

지나간 일들은 하나씩
길목을 지키는 술래가 된다.

After a farewell

At this time, newly
Reaching out their hands,
The landscape of mountains and fields.

By wrapping all of the stories
I fathom the smoked time.

One by one, the things that have passed
Becoming a tagger who guards the street corner.

여름날 그때 그곳에

산기슭 외딴 집 마당에
구름 한 자락 잡아놓고

나이 들수록 또렷해지는
삭힌 생각이나
구겨 버린 시구詩句의 아쉬움이
다시 살아 오른다.

오늘은 어떤 일이
일어나고 있을까.

불빛 찾아
어디선가 풍뎅이가 날아와
일깨우는 말

하늘 끝의
바람과 구름을 바라보란다.

On a summer day there

In the yard of an isolated house on the mountain slope
Catching one edge of the clouds

What becomes clear as I get older
Fermented thoughts or
The inconvenience of the crumpled verse is
Rising alive again.

What kind of happening is
Occurring today?

For finding the light
A beetle flies here from somewhere, then
The reminding words

It tells me to look at the winds and clouds
At the end of the sky.

피끝 냇가

손을 담가
푸른 하늘을 움키다가
감색 옷고름만 뜯긴
첫사랑을 그리워 하다가
토담집 담장에 온몸 비틀거리며
꽃 그늘에 숨었던
그림자를 펴 본다.

불에 탄 고목이
아직도 그을린 채
뜨거운 열기를 품었다가
죽계竹溪 시냇가에 가지를 드리우고
세월을 지탱하는 건

안개를 걷어내는 햇살이
열린 차창을 넘어 들어와

귀엣말로
순흥順興고을 냇물에 얼비친
서원철폐 바람에도 끄떡 않던
나그네 봇짐을 풀어보라 한다.

On a summer day there

In the yard of an isolated house on the mountain slope
Catching one edge of the clouds

What becomes clear as I get older
Fermented thoughts or
The inconvenience of the crumpled verse is
Rising alive again.

What kind of happening is
Occurring today?

For finding the light
A beetle flies here from somewhere, then
The reminding words

It tells me to look at the winds and clouds
At the end of the sky.

피끝 냇가

손을 담가
푸른 하늘을 움키다가
감색 옷고름만 뜯긴
첫사랑을 그리워 하다가
토담집 담장에 온몸 비틀거리며
꽃 그늘에 숨었던
그림자를 펴 본다.

불에 탄 고목이
아직도 그을린 채
뜨거운 열기를 품었다가
죽계竹溪 시냇가에 가지를 드리우고
세월을 지탱하는 건

안개를 걷어내는 햇살이
열린 차창을 넘어 들어와

귀엣말로
순흥順興고을 냇물에 얼비친
서원철폐 바람에도 끄떡 않던
나그네 봇짐을 풀어보라 한다.

A stream in the Pikkeut village

Dipping my hands
Grabbing the blue sky
Missing my first love
That the navy string of clothes is torn out,
Staggering my whole body on the wall of a mud house
Hidden in the flower shade
I spread that shadow.

The burnt old tree
Still scorched
Holding the heat and
Hanging down branches along the Jukgye stream,
What it sustains the years

The sunshine which is skimming the fog
Comes across the open window

With a whisper
Glimmering on the stream of Sunheung Village,
Ask to unpack the traveler's luggage
That it had endured to the abolition period of traditional auditoriums.

추녀 밑으로 달빛이 들 때
황소 같은 성글한 눈망울들
갑옷 차려 입고 내죽리內竹里에서

꽃잎으로 떨어져
액서가 남았으리.

When the moonlight comes under the eaves
Those grinning eyeballs like a yellow cow,
Dressed up in armor at the Naejuk-ri

Falling as petals
There must be left a signboard.

소박데기

꽃모종을 서두르던 시절
하찮은 푸념 때문에
남 몰래 삭이는 얼굴.

헛눈 팔고 지내온 나날들이
어쩌면 나를 잃게 하고 만 것일까.

저마다 배당된 하루에
삶의 빛깔을 윤내던
이치와 억지 같은 것.

이제 다시
마구 흐트러진 더벅머리에
거울 속의 바람은
어떤 예감에 응어리져 있을까.

우세를 사는 골목에서
젖은 내 안색을 날린다.

이제사 너에게서
저녁노을이 물드는 이유를 알았다.

A deserted wife

The season when the seeding of flowers is in a hurry
Because of trivial complaints,
A face of swallowing its emotions secretly.

The days I've been distracted,
Might it made me lose myself?

To the allocated day to each one
Shining the color of life
Something like principle and stubbornness.

Now again
On my hair that gets disheveled
The wind in the mirror,
To what kind of premonition is it pressured?

In the alley where is mocked
Blowing away my wet complexion.

Finally, from you
I knew why the evening glow was coloring.

대부도 여신女神

유두봉 그늘은
여염집 가시내로 버티어 서 있다.
아지랑이가 치맛자락을 걷어 올리면
수줍은 몸짓은 더 유연하다.

세속의 미련 때문에
고개 젖히고
뱃고동소리에 발돋움할 뿐,

전설은 고즈넉한 사랑
너의 한 허리에 집을 짓고
살아온 백성에게
이제는 돌아가라 하는가.

그 어디에도
대답은 없구나.

The goddess of Daebu Island

The shade of Yudu Peak
Withstands as a girl of commoner's house.
When the haze rolls up the end of the skirt,
Her bashful gesture is more flexible.

Because of worldly attachment,
Tilting her head back
Just stands on tiptoe for the sound of a boat horn,

The legend builds a house
On the cozy love, one part of your waist and
Does it tell the people who have lived to go back now?

Nowhere
There's no answer.

탈속脫俗

잠겨 있는 문밖에서
편지를 읽으면
수척한 나의 손은
물기어린 넝쿨로 자란다.

이마를 짚고
무성한 하늘로 날으는 의식들이
와르를 모여 와
나를 에워싼다.

무엇을 갖는다는 건
소중함을 마중하는 것인가.

빛내고 싶던
튼튼한 내 덧니
나는 그저 흙으로밖에 비유되지 않았다.

사람으로 선택되어
사람이어야 하는데
미물들이 눈을 뜨는 시각이면
이미 나는 사람이 아니다.

Unworldliness

Outside the locked door
If I read a letter,
My haggard hands
Grow as watery vines.

After touching on the forehead
Flying consciousness toward the exuberant sky,
Gathering around with rush and
Surround me.

To have something is,
Is it to greet the precious thing?

What I want to shine is
My strong protruding tooth
I have been compared to only soil.

Chosen as a person,
I should be a person, but
When minikins open their eyes,
I am not a person already.

다시, 출발점에서

그 깊으나 깊은 곳에
수척한 눈 그늘
비록 웃는 모습에서도
서러움의 껍질이 포개져 있지.
나도 모르게 마음이 자꾸 변절해 가듯이
내 삶의 숱한 입김이
언제나 내 가까이서 서걱거리듯이
쓰고 지운 흔적뿐인 것을
얼마나 애틋한 음률로
나의 어둠을 고동쳤는가.
백지 속에 잠적한
나의 자유여.

Again, at the starting point

Where it's deep and deep
The gaunt shade of eyes,
Even on the smiling face
The skin of sorrow is folded there.
As my mind changing without my awareness,
Like always crunching near to me
Plentiful breaths of my life are
The only traces of writing and erasing
With how pathetic melodies,
Did it throb my darkness?
That vanishes in a blank paper,
Dear my freedom.

바람은

바람은
푸른 들판을 달릴 때도
아무 생각을 않는다.

바람은
무리 속의 자기를
더욱 알지 못한다.

바람은
돌층계를 오르는
먼동의 신음을 토할 뿐,

바람은 언제나
바람으로 잠버릇을 같이 한다.

바람은
오직 자기를 버리지 않고 챙긴다.

The wind is

The wind is,
When it runs through the green field,
It thinks nothing.

The wind is,
It doesn't know itself more
Among its crowds.

The wind is,
It just emits a groan of far dawn
Which climbs on stone stairs.

The wind is always
Along with sleeping habit with the wind.

The wind is,
It takes care of only itself without abandoning itself.

제2부 Part 2

그리움은 숨어 살고 기다림은 울며 산다
Longing lives in hiding and waiting lives in crying

아득한 해안선 따라
구름이 달려가고
바람이 달려가도
어디로 가는지 묻지 않았다.
- 「어느 서해안 선에서」 중에서

Along the distant coastline
The clouds run and
The winds run, but
I didn't ask where they were going.
- The part of 「At one west coastline」

사랑할 때

수채화 화폭 속에
번지는 그림자.

내 지탱해 온 사랑은
거듭나는 되풀이.

생각이 익고 있는 능금밭에서
벽 하나를 허물고
뒤돌아서면
나는 봄을 타는 식성으로 어른이 되어
들바람이 서성이는 귀로에
나부끼는 풀잎.

너에게 손님으로 묵고 있는
나의 마중,
어둠은 나의 돌아앉은 몸짓이었다.

When in love

Inside the picture of watercolor painting
A spreading shadow.

My sustaining love is
The repetition of rebirth.

On the apple farm where thoughts are ripe
When I abolish one of the walls
And return,
Becoming a grown-up with food habit of getting spring fever
On the backtrack where fields wind hovers,
I am grass leaves with flapping.

My coming to meet,
That is staying as a guest with you
The darkness was a gesture of turning my back.

빛의 숨결

살아있는 것
자연이 알아서
대가 없이 키워준 것

어느 날
새벽을 오려내어 어둠을 덮으며

언뜻언뜻 회오리바람에 쓸리는 것.

The breath of light

Living thing,
Nature brings up it
By itself, without a price

One day
Covering the darkness after cutting the dawn

Being swept away by a whirlwind in a flash.

바닷가 아침에

파도에 떠밀려

구름 속으로 숨었다가

마당가 꽃그늘에 앉아

파란 하늘을 가득 그렸다.

By the sea in the morning

Pushed by the waves

Hiding in the cloud,

Sitting in the flower shade in the yard

And I painted the blue sky full.

바람의 침묵 · 1

대문 빗장은 걸리고
별들이 삭정이에 널려 있을 때
바람은 수채구로 기어 나왔다
외딴 길목에서 낯익은 목소리 들려오고
하늘이 지워진 밤에
바람을 은폐시킬 방도가 없었다
소나무 두어 그루 둘러앉은
두엄더미로 몸을 숨겼다
바람의 빛깔과 하늘의 무게가
늪으로 빠져들었다
소나무 밑동을 검잡고 숨죽일 때
설레임과 침묵이 한 묶음이었다.

The silence of the wind · 1

The door latch was locked and
When the stars were spread on dead branches,
The wind crawled out toward the drain
The familiar voice is heard from the isolated street corner and
On the night when the sky was erased,
There was no way to cover up the wind
It hid itself into the compost heap
Seated around about two pine trees
The color of the wind and the weight of the sky
Fell into the swamp
When holding breath with grabbing the stump of a pine tree,
Trembling and silence were a bundle.

# 바람의 침묵 · 2

검부럭지 범벅된 늪에서
한 짝 신을 벗긴 채 바람은 기어 나왔다
나무다리가 뒷짐 지고 서있는 개울가에서는
차라리 어떠한 한기도 느끼지 못했다
횅한 귓속을 맴도는 훈훈한 입김
칠흑 같은 침묵
영원할 것만 같은 밤이었다.

The silence of the wind · 2

In the swamp where the remnants are messed up
The wind crawled out with one shoe off
By the brook where the wooden bridge stands with
its hands clasped behind its back,
Rather nor a chill was found
A balmy breath that lingers in the deserted ear
The silence as coal black
It seemed like an eternal night.

바른 말

오지랖 잎새

하늘 가리고

빈정거림에 떨어지다.

An outspoken right word

A meddlesome leaf

Hiding the sky

Falls by innuendo.

박꽃바람

눈물 쏟을 것 같은 그
눈빛으로

몸살 하던 밤
하얀 상념 한 아름 안고

달밤과
나누던 얘기
왜 입 다물었나.

An outspoken right word

A meddlesome leaf

Hiding the sky

Falls by innuendo.

박꽃바람

눈물 쏟을 것 같은 그
눈빛으로

몸살 하던 밤
하얀 상념 한 아름 안고

달밤과
나누던 얘기
왜 입 다물었나.

The gourd flower wind

With the eyeshine
That is about to shed tears

The night when it ached all its body,
Holding an armful of white thoughts

A shared story
With the moonlight
Why does it button up its lip?

독도에게

쪽빛 바다
절반은 애련

아득한 시간
절반은 연민

낯익은 뱃고동소리에
뒷모습으로 우두커니 서서

내심 반겨주는
너

풀꽃들만 인적을 그리워했으랴
물안개만 삭신을 애착했으랴

오늘을 살아가는 물그림자에
별들은 쏟아져 내리고
내게로 다가와 헤살 짓는
너

To Dokdo Island

The indigo blue sea
The half is plaintiveness

A distant time
The half is compassion

At the familiar boat horn sound
Standing absently as an appearance in the back

Inwardly greeting
You

Did only the grass flowers long for the human's trace?
Did only wet fog feel an attachment to the sinews and joints?

On the water shadow that lives today
The starts pour and
Coming closer to me and taunting,
You

섬
섬
섬
모국어.

Island

Island

Island

Mother tongue.

바람 속에서

얼마나 오랜만에 찾아온 대면인가
아름 재던 아카시아 비슷이 서성이고
오월의 바람은
푸른 숨소리를 가슴에 쏟아 붓는다

우이동 산촌山村에
햇살을 휘젓고 찾아 갔더니
풀냄새만 그득하더라.

웃자란 찔래순을 꺾어
어린 시절을 뇌어본다
순한 풋내음은 입 안 가득
달빛 같기도 하여
부끄러운 눈빛으로 속다짐하다가
초라한 혈색으로
뉘엿대는 그림자 따라
하늘 속으로 숨는다.

산이 말 없이 따라와
풀꽃으로 서성인다
휘청이는 것은
풀꽃 사이 가득한 바람이더라.

In the wind

How long has it been since then?
The acacia flower which measures its beauty hangs
out obliquely
The wind of May
Pours blue breaths into the chest

To the mountain village in the Ui-dong
I visited there with stirring sunshine, then
It smelled grasses fully there.

Broken the sprout of a wild rose which grows uselessly,
I reflect upon my childhood
Full of mild fresh scents in my mouth
Seems like moonlight
So, I make myself a promise with a shy glance
With my poor complexion
Along with shadow of slow sinking
I hide in the sky.

The mountain follows silently and
It hangs out as grass flowers
What is swaying is
That was the wind that's full among the grass flowers.

안부·1
−친구 안이모에게

안형
잊고 지낸 동안 새로워졌나 보네
문득 떠오른 간밤은
모처럼 지루한 밤이 아니었네
어떻게 사는지 궁금하지 않았네
내 모습을 유리창에 비춰보니
그 속에 빙긋이 웃고 있었네.

안형, 나 송전松田일세
뭐라, 의정부 솔밭이란 말이네
응, 살아 있읍네
아니, 저승에서 전화하는 거 아닌가
아니 이 인간아, 어디로 잠적했었나
그래 그 인간아, 내 말을 왜 써먹나

사십여 년의 세월에도
식어버리지 않은 지열로
기막힌 입맛은 살아 있네.

Best Regards · 1

- To my friend Ahn Eee-mo

Brother Ahn
Looks like you've been renewed while I forgot
Last night that suddenly came to my mind,
It wasn't a long boring night for a change
I didn't wonder how you're doing
When I saw myself through the window,
I was laughing around in it.

Brother Ahn, I'm Song Jeon
What? It means Uijeongbu pine field
Yes, I'm alive
What! Aren't you calling from the underworld?
Oh, man, where have you been hiding?
Yeah, man, why are you using my words?

Even in the forty years
Due to geothermal heat that has not cooled down
Your amazing golden tongue is alive.

어떻게 변했을까
이승에 아직 자빠져 있을까
참으로 몹쓸 인간이야
보고 싶으면 찾아볼 일이지
무슨 일 바빠 삭히는가.

독백의 밤은 고요하네.

How have you been changed?
Are you still fallen in this world?
You're a very bad man
If you want to meet me, you can look for me, but
What makes you busy with restraining from doing?

The night of monologues is quiet.

침묵

마음 안에서 홀로 숨쉬며

무엇이라도 씻어 새로움을 빚는 것.

Silence

Breathing alone in my mind

It's creating new by washing anything.

어느 서해안 선에서

모래에 파묻힌 해당화
나팔꽃이 휘감고 어울렸다
촘촘한 가시 사이로 넝쿨을 뻗어
바다 안개 머금은 아침이다.

아득한 해안선 따라
구름이 달려가고
바람이 달려가도
어디로 가는지 묻지 않았다.

언제 보아도
모래 속에 발목을 묻으면
나는 썰물로 빠져나간다.

해당화는 해당화로
나팔꽃은 나팔꽃으로
해안선을 따라 핀다.

At one west coastline

The Rosa rugosa buried by the sand,
The morning glory twisted it and got along with it
Spreading vines between the dense thorns,
It's a morning with holding sea fog.

Along the distant coastline
The clouds run and
The winds run, but
I didn't ask where they were going.

Whenever I see
If I bury my ankles in the sand,
I am escaping as an ebb tide.

Rosa rugosa is as a Rosa rugosa
Morning glory is as a morning glory
They bloom along the coastline.

백문서원

소백산 한 허리로
피어오르는 물안개
하늘과 땅을 가꾸고 다스려
순흥 고을에 아침을 차려 놓는다

당신의 인생사
물속에 갈앉은 가랑잎에도
시원의 뜻을 깨치게끔
옛날 그대로 여기 있는데

계곡은 더욱 계곡으로 깊어지고
이제도 그대로 폐허로 남아 있는
마을 어귀에
풀들만 파릇한 냄새를 풍기고 있다

백문서원을 세운 열정은
계곡에 남아 있지만
안개가 장막처럼 가려져 있다.

Baekmun traditional auditorium

On its waist part of Sobaek mountain
Rising mist is
Cultivating and governing the sky and the earth and
Prepares breakfast in Sunheung Village

Your life story,
Even on dead leaves that sank into the water
For realizing the meaning of origin,
It's here the way it used to be and
The valley gets deeper into the valley,
Now remains as ruinous as it is
At the entrance to the village
Only the grasses are giving out fresh scents

The passion that established the Baekmun traditional auditorium
Still remains in the valley, but
The fog is shrouded like a curtain.

귀 향

장독대 빈자리엔
접시꽃이 주인이다

헛기침에 고개 들어
그늘 드린 구름을 본다
모두가 타인이다

한밤을 헤쳐
고백하려는 두려움으로
아슴한 순간에 젖는다.

삶이 무언지도 모르고
생활로 무르익은 나는
부끄러움에 몸부림친다.

언제나 나는
골목을 휘젓던 바람이었다.

굴욕에 젖은 손을 씻고
세상 사노라며
아픔을 잊으리라.

Returning home

In the empty place of crocks
A hollyhock is an owner

After a small cough with lifting my face
Looking up the shadowy clouds
Everyone is a stranger

Through the midnight
In the fear of confession,
Get wet at a vague moment.

I am totally immature of what life is
But mature to livelihood,
Trembled at that shame.

Always I've been,
The wind that swept the alley.

Washing my wet hands from humiliation and
I will live life and
Forget the pain.

세월 아득히

구름 한 다발 꺾어서

세월 아득히

한 조각 뜯어 날리다.

Afar the years

Breaking a bunch of clouds,

The years afar

Tearing off one piece and fly it away.

그리움 일랴

아무리 잡아당겨도
회오리바람 속으로 휘말려버리는
모든 시간의 정제

굴래 속에
아직도 떠나지 않고
옛날로 남아 있는 것.

그리움 일랴
땅거미인 듯 그림자를 드리워

그 언젠가 어둠이 선잠을 깨워주던
그때 그대로 사방에 흩어져서
무겁게 어깨를 짓누르고
오늘도
모양새 갖추어 다가온다.

다시 잊을 수만 있다면 날리고 싶다.

The longing is

No matter how much I pull it,
Being swept into a tornado,
The purification of all time

Inside the confines
Still not leaving,
What remains as old times.

The longing is
Casting a shadow as if twilight

One day, just as when the darkness awakened me to a light sleep
It is scattered everywhere,
Pressing my shoulder heavily
Today as well,
It comes closer with preparing its shape.

I want to fly it if I can forget it again.

제3부 Part 3

이별의 뒤란에서 해후의 뜨락으로

From the back of farewell to the garden of a meeting

꽃그늘을 베고 비슷이 누워
바람의 향기를 맡는다
나도 하늘도 꽃이슬로 남는다.
- 「꽃과 삶」 중에서

Laying down obliquely with my head in the flower shade
I smell the fragrance of the wind
Both I and the sky remain as flower dew.
- The part of 「Flowers and life」

바람 속으로

실로 삼십여 년 만에
나 혼자 약속으로 기차를 탔다.

멀리 날려버린 바람
앙상한 나목으로 날 세워 두고

아무 일도 없었다는 듯
마주 바라보는 차창에
떠오르는 얼굴이 새삼 선명하다.

짙은 안개 속으로 산언덕을 오르다
빈 들을 가로질러 간다.

차창에 어리는 달빛이
나의 원형을 기억해내려
남아 있는 여백을 찾는다.
이제는 모든 것을
그대로 남겨두고 싶다.

Into the winds

Indeed, after around 30 years
I took the train on my own appointment.

The wind that blows away
Puts me stand as a skinny bare tree and

As if nothing had happened
On the faced train window
The rising face is clear anew.

Climbing the mountain hill in the thick fog, then
I am crossing the empty field.

The moonlight what is glimmering
To remember my original form
Finds the remained spare.
Now everything
I want to leave it as it is.

백 자

오랜 가슴앓이 끝에
푸르게 가슴 가득히 안아 지녔다.

전생의 하늘이랄까,
내세의 하늘이랄까.

서리고 서린 하늘 속에서
여인이 걸어 나오는 모습.

오늘의 찌든 숨결을
가을 하늘빛으로 헹구어
얼비치는 속살 깊이로
번져오는 풍금소리다.

A white porcelain

After a long heartburn
Heartily embracing it in blue.

Might it be the sky of a prior life?
Might it be the sky of the afterlife?

From the mistily misty sky
The shape that a woman comes out.

The ingrained breath of today
Rinsing it in the color of the autumn sky
Into the depth of subtly visible skin
It's the spreading sound of a reed organ.

흘러가는 구름을 바라보며

아직 남아있는 것들을 챙겨
이제 또 어디로 갈까.

내 나이 육십
흘려보내던 나를 줍는다.

내버렸던 것 중에 하나하나
추슬러 바람에 날린다.

돌 틈새에 뿌리 드러낸 풀 한 포기
올려다본다.

그래도 아직 남아있는 그리움
무엇으로 삭힐 수 있으랴.

Looking at the flowing clouds

Preparing what is still left
Where will I go again now?

My age is sixty
I pick up me who I was sending.

Each one of the things I've thrown away
Blow it after picking and trimming.

One clump of grass that has revealed its root in the crevice of the stone
I look up.

The longing that still remains
With what can it be calmed down?

물속에서 흔들린다

산골짜기 논두렁길을 질러가다
논물 가둬 놓은 논바닥에 드리운 그림자
물속에서 흔들린다.

논두렁을 지나
시절의 유년도 지나
한곳에 머물지 못하고 멀리 떠나와 지내는 자리
흘러가는 물을 바라본다.

가만히 정지해 있던 것이 모두 살아나
메아리로 들리는 한낮에
하얀 찔레꽃을 바라본다.

걷다가 달리다가
뛰다가 주저앉아 보아도 제 모습이다.

거친 들바람에
무슨 속엣 말을 전하겠는가.

Sways in the water

Traversing a rice paddy road in the mountain valley
The cast shadow in the soil of a rice paddy where the waters are stored,
It sways in the water.

Has passed across a rice paddy road and
Passed the childhood, then
The place where I stay after departing afar without stays one spot,
I see that water flowing.

The quietly stopped things are all revived
At midday when it is heard as an echo
I see a white wild rose.

However, walking and running,
Jumping and flopping down, but it's my own appearance.

To the rough field wind
What kind of inward word do I say?

빛의 울림을 그린다

텅 빈 바람 속에
언제라도 들여다보며
바람 앞에서
빛의 울림을 그린다.

살았다는 고귀함은
그림자의 모습이 아니다.

풀잎에 맺힌 이슬방울 하나로
온갖 속내를 닦았으면 한다.

누군가도 질러갔을 이 지평에서
시를 쓰며
아픔을 어루만진다.

거기 나의 모습이 떠오른다.
바람 앞에서
빛의 울림이다.

I draw the echoes of light

In the empty wind
Looking at any time
In front of the wind
I draw the echoes of light.

The nobility of living a life,
It's not the shape of the shadow.

With one drop of dew formed on grass leaf
I hope to wipe the entire inward mind.

On the horizon where anyone could have crossed
Writing poetry
I caress my pain.

There, my appearance is rising.
In front of the wind
It's the echoes of light.

어느 날

침묵 한 켠에서
엽서를 쓴다.

한마디 말에도
한없이 일렁이는
아득함.

멀고 가까움이 어디 있고
안과 밖이 따로 없다.

One day

At one corner of silence
I write a postcard.

From even a word
Swaying limitlessly
Farness.

Where are farness and closeness?
There's no separation between the inside and outside.

너와의 걸음걸이

푸념의 속살을 감추고
낯선 그림자와 동행하면서
나를 잠행한다.

밤을 뒤척이게 하는 수많은 습성 가운데
손발 저리도록 무엇인가 떨리어
나를 깜박 잃는다.

자유라는 파란 잎새로
어디서 내가
억지를 부리고 있는 걸까.

너울 속을 휘젓고
밤새 사라진 꿈에서
지금은 무슨 기억을 쓸고 있는 것인지.

서릿발을 밟고 파묻은
기억을 키우는데
뿌리 뽑힌 나무의 어지러움을
누가 알랴.

Walking with you

Hiding the bare skin of complaints,
Along with an unfamiliar shadow
I am going undercover.

Among the many habits which make the night toss and turn
Something shakes to numb my hands and feet
So, I lose my mind.

With a green leaf named freedom
Where do I
Persist stubbornly?

Stirring inside of the big wave and
In the disappeared dream all night,
What kind of memory do I sweep away now?

Stepping on the needle of ice and burying it
I grow that memory
Who knows the dizziness of the tree
That its roots are pulled out?

눈에 어른거리는
그리움을 몰고 가는 저 푸르름
거기, 너와의 걸음걸이.

Glimmering in my eyes,
The green that is driving longing
There, walking with you.

폐교 운동장

산그늘만 마중 나온 폐교 운동장
잡초보다 키 작은 코스모스가
풍금소리에 하늘거린다.

비에 씻긴 비탈에 서서
안개이슬 먹고 버텨 온 코스모스
꽃씨 여물게 몸부림친다.

깨진 유리창 공간엔 거미줄 치고
울고 있는 누이의 손에
녹슨 종소리가 꽃이다.

The playground of a closed school

The playground of a closed school where only a mountain shadow welcomes
The short cosmos than weeds are
Wavering by the sound of an organ.

Standing on the slope, washed by rain
The cosmos, that is sustained by eating the foggy dew
Struggles for the ripening of flower seeds.

Weaving a web on the space of a broken window and
In the hands of a crying sister
The sound of a rusty bell is a flower.

종소리와 비천상

한순간에
하늘에서 내려오는 자태
새벽 산사의 종소리는
은은한 여운으로 나뭇잎 하나에도 부딪침 없다.

경내에 어둠은
종소리에 먼동이 터 온다.

종소리가 나뭇잎에 내려앉을 때
바람은 자기 모습을 본다.
구름 속에
나는 종소리와 거기 스며들었다.

The sound of a bell and the image of a flying fairy

In a moment of time
The appearance of descending from the sky
The sound of a bell from the mountain temple of dawn,
There's no crash to even a leaf with delicate after sound.

Darkness in the precinct,
It dawns on the sound of the bell.

When the sound of a bell falls on the leaves,
The wind looks at itself.
In the clouds
I am permeated there with the sound of the bell.

어느 이국 하늘 아래서도

낯선 이국에서도
마음 속 눈길 하나까지
생각도 바뀌고 관점도 되잡아
다듬어야지.

계절이 바뀌고
하늘이 바뀌어도
속내 깊이 간직한 무엇이라도
모두 바뀌어 가는 순리이겠지만

어린 시절 밤을 새우며 바라보던
하늘을 다시 보아라
그 하늘의 은하수를 헤아려 보아라.

어느 세월의 굽이일망정
네 눈뜨는 자리가
바로 하늘인 것을 새겨라.

Under a foreign sky also

Even in a foreign country
Even one eye glance of the inner mind
I change also the thought and catch again the point of view,
I will trim it.

The season changes and
Even if the sky changes,
Whatever cherishing it in the deep inner mind,
It's the reasonableness that everything is changing, but

The sky where you had looked all night when childhood,
Look at that sky again
Count the Milky Way of that sky.

Even it's the curve of certain times
The place where your eyes open, It's right the sky
Engrave it in your heart.

바람의 말 · 2

나뭇가지마다 초록 잎새
바람이 건네주는 말
'꿈이야'
남긴 여운 한가운데
꽃의 손길은 무엇일까.
말은 들리지 않지만
꿈 언저리에서
'하늘이야'
모든 것이 뒤덮이는 어둠 속에서
나는 눈을 뜬다.

떠도는 형상이 하늘에 가득하다.
밟힌 그림자
하얀 그림자
강둑엔 안개가 이슬로 내린다.

누가 바람을 탓하지는 않겠지만
바람은 푸르른 말씨를 고른다.

The words of the wind · 2

Green leaves on every branch
Words from the wind,
'It's a dream'
In the middle of a lingering atmosphere
What's the touch of the flower?
That word is inaudible, but
Around of dream,
'It's the sky'
In the darkness, where everything is covered
I open my eyes.

The lingering images are full in the sky.
The trampled shadow
The white shadow
The fog descends as dew on the riverbank.

Nobody blames the wind, but
The wind chooses a blue tone for the words.

소용돌이 속에서

동이 터 오면
하늘이 덤벙거린다.

잘 익은 노을 속에서
솎아 낸
묶음의 세상이 흙발로 덤벙거린다.

아양을 가꾸고 가리던 푸릇한 말씨들이
입덧 한 자락을 깨물며 덤벙거린다.

녹슨 문고리에
매어 달린 고통이
채색된 유리로 덤벙거린다.

관념의 아침저녁
빛깔과 알몸이 덤벙거린다
손금의 도랑에서 한 시절을 덤벙거린다.

In the whirlpool

When dawn comes,
The sky moves carelessly.

In the well ripe sunset
The world of the bundle, that is pulled out sparsely
Moves carelessly with dirty feet.

The bluish accents that have decorated and sorted out flattery
Moves carelessly with biting a part of morning sickness.

On a rusty doorknob
The hanging anguish
Moves carelessly as painted ethics.

The morning and evening of concept
The color and the bare body move carelessly,
Move carelessly a time of life on the ditch of palm's line.

꽃과 삶

꽃은 토양을 가리지 않고
일조권이나 기후 풍토를 탓하지 않는다.

꽃은 본디 심성으로
스스로 조절한다.

비탈진 바위 틈새에 뿌리를 더 활착시키고
앙증스러운 몸짓일망정
낮게 구부린 등덜미며
가냘픈 손바닥들이
꽃의 참모습이다

꽃은 그림자처럼 따르며
자기의 속성을 바꿀 뿐이다

꽃은 새로움이 없다고 말하지 말자
순하게 살아온 모든 것들이
어리석고 나약한 숨소리로 기가 꺾여도
정말이지 새것이 아니라고 우기지 말자

Flowers and life

Flowers don't distinguish soils
And not to blame the right of sunlight or climate.

Flowers control for themselves
With their own nature.

More rooting in the crevice of sloping rock and
Even a dainty gesture
With a low bent back
And the delicate palms
They are the true face of flowers

The flowers are followed like shadows and
Just change their nature

Let's not say flowers have no novelty
All those that have lived gently,
Although they are discouraged by foolish and feeble breath,
In very truth, let's not insist they are not new

꽃그늘을 베고 비슷이 누워
바람의 향기를 맡는다
나도 하늘도 꽃이슬로 남는다.

꽃은 언제나 그대로이다
그 또한 탓하지 않는다.
꽃은 제 모습 그대로일 뿐이다.

Laying down obliquely with my head in the flower shade
I smell the fragrance of the wind
Both I and the sky remain as flower dew.

The flowers are always as they are
They don't blame it also.
They are just the shape they are.

어떤 기다림

지금 이 순간
오랜 밤바다를 지켜보는
안개밭.

목쉰 바람이
파도로 다가와 넘실대다가
허황한 한밤을 일깨운다.

미련과 고독의
너울을 바라보는
장승의 하염없는 눈매

안간힘의 몸부림으로
나를 비탈에 세우는 것은
삭일 수 없는 그리움 때문이다
떨쳐버릴 수 없는 그림자 때문이다.

A certain wait

In this moment
Watching the old sea at night,
The fog field

A hoarse wind
Comes as waves and rolling over,
Awakens the hollow midnight.

Of lingering attachment and solitude
Watching the heaving sea,
The totem pole's endless glance

In a desperate struggle
Erecting me on the slope,
It's because of unappeasable longing
It's because of the undetached shadow.

연꽃 소묘

연록 빛으로 뒤덮인 회산연꽃단지의 개구리 풀은
연꽃과 연잎 아래
꿇어 엎드린 형상이라.

뿌리줄기를 박차고
수면 위로 주먹을 쥐고 솟아오르며
푸른 하늘과 바람
포근한 햇빛과 향기를 품고
말없이 꿇어 엎드린 개구리뿐

꼭 쥔 주먹을 물 위의 파문에 닿지 않게 끌어올려
천천히 주먹을 편다.

할 말이 또렷하게
내 안에 남기고 갔는가.

몇 겹으로 두른 꽃잎 속
뿌리의 떫은맛을 삭히고
꽃 턱의 구멍 속에 씨를 품었는가.
흰 분홍빛 얼굴로 내 머리맡에 나앉아
노을에 꽃잎을 벙글어
밤을 밝히는가.

The sketch of a lotus

Duckweed of the Hoesan lotus park, which is covered with light green
Under the lotus and lotus leaves
It is a figure of kneeling down.

Kicking the stem of the root
Rising with a clenching fist over the surface
The blue sky and the wind
Holding warm sunshine and its fragrance
Only a silent fog that kneeled and faced down

Hoisting a handfast fist for not touching the ripples on the water
Slowly opens its fist.

Had it clearly left
The words to say to me and go?

In petals which are wrapped with several layers
Soothing the acerbity of its root and
Does it bear the seed in the hole of the flower's receptacle?
Seating out beside my head with a white, pink face
Having petal bud at dusk and
Does it light up the night?

봄 흙으로 젖어 계세요
- 서인수 교육장님의 정년퇴임에 부쳐

시골 장터의 풍물과 함께 동화되어
사십 성상 외길로
허물을 사랑하고
서로를 나누어 가진 하늘.

모나지 않고
모습에서부터 목소리에 젖어
하늘로 닿는 인정이 살가롭기만 하다.

서투른 풍금소리에 휘파람도 불고
무지개 잡으러 찰랑이던 종이배 띄우시고
황톳길 신작로 가로질러
지평선을 밟고 서서
봄 흙으로 젖어 거기 그대로 계세요.

초등학교 그 날로부터 운동장에는
흐리지 않은 눈빛들이
줌과 받음의 오롯함으로,

Please stay wet with spring soil
-To the retirement of Superintendent of Education Seo In-soo

Assimilated with the folklore of the rural marketplace
By a single path for forty years
In love with the faults
The sky that shared each other.

Without being angulate
Being wet from appearance to voice
The warm heart that reaches the sky is only affectionate.

Whistling to the clumsy organ sound and
Floating the paper boat that used to catch the rainbow,
Across newly constructed red clay road and
Standing on the horizon,
Please stay there with wetting by spring soil.

From that day of elementary school, on the playground
Eyes that are not clouded
With the fullness of giving and receiving,

중등학교가 하 오래된 길손이어서
우러러 그리웠던 우리의 동행
지순한 시간이여!

이날껏 장학으로
흙을 뭉개주고 줄기를 걷어 올려
가꾸고 다스림이여!

이제 다시 시작해도 좋겠으니
질러가는 길로 가지 마시고
지금 막 트인 길로만 가까이 다가가세요.

꽃받침이 꽃씨를 싸안듯
초록빛 매무새로 두고두고 창창하세요.

Since middle school is, ah, an old traveler,
Our companion that we respected and missed,
Dear innocent time!

Encouragement of learning until this time
Crushing the soil and rolling up the stem,
Dear caring and governing!

Starting over is okay now
Don't go ahead on the road
Just get closer to the open road.

As if a calyx wraps a flower seed,
Leave it as a green shape and keep it fresh ever.

제4부 Part 4

보내고 나면 돌아오는 것들
Things that come back after sending

다 주고 빈손으로 서서
바람이 요동쳐도 그대로
구름의 이끌림에도 그 자리에 서 있는
한 그루 나무
- 「겨울나무 · 2」 중에서

Standing with empty hands after giving everything
Although the wind fluctuates, but still as it is,
Standing in that place even to the attraction of the clouds
A winter tree
- The part of 「A winter tree · 2」

하늘 아래서

하루를 깨어나면서부터
바람을 마주하고
휘둘리지 않으려 안간힘 다 하는 시작이다.

가진 것 다 갖고도 풍요로움 없는 이 밤에
무슨 고백을 해야 하는가
어둠 속에서 나를 찾는다.

무엇으로도 비유할 수 없는 형상이
내 안 깊이 다시 떠올라 새긴다.

동행의 그림자와
오늘도 하늘 아래서
가까이 길을 간다.

Under the sky

From waking up the day
Facing the winds,
It's the beginning of making utmost efforts not to be wielded.

On this night without abundance even with everything I have
What kind of confession should I make?
I am finding myself in the dark.

The figure that can compare to nothing
Rises again deep inside me and carved in.

Along with the accompanying shadow
Today again, under the sky
I am going near the road.

겨울나무 · 2

눈 쌓인 산길에
겨울나무는 튼튼하다.

다 주고 빈손으로 서서
바람이 요동쳐도 그대로
구름의 이끌림에도 그 자리에 서 있는
한 그루 나무

추녀 끝 풍경이 바람을 탄다.
풍경소리가 하늘과 땅을
고요 속에 품어 안는다.

겨울나무가 산을 지키고
산은 눈 속에 묻힌다.

나도 한 그루
겨울나무가 되고 싶다.

A winter tree · 2

On a snowy mountain way
A winter tree is strong.

Standing with empty hands after giving everything
Although the wind fluctuates, but still as it is,
Standing in that place even to the attraction of the clouds
A winter tree

The scenery of eaves rides the winds.
Its sound embraces
The sky and the ground in silence.

The winter tree guards the mountain
And the mountain is buried under snow.

I hope to be
A winter tree.

호수와 달과 산

호수에 달이 흔들린다.
물가에서 바라보다가
나뭇가지로 휘저어 본다.

일렁이는 달빛이
사방으로 퍼져간다.
빛살의 무늬가 아득히 멀어진다.

호수 속 달이
산을 안개로 감싸 안는다.

정적의 한가운데
별들이 소복이 내려오고
나는 흘러간 시간을 마주하고
마지막 별 하나를 줍는다.

The lake, the moon, and the mountain

The moon shakes on the lake
Looking it at the lakeside,
I try stirring it with a twig.

The rocking moonlights are
Spreading everywhere.
The pattern of light drifts apart far away.

The moon in the lake
Embraces the mountain with fog.

In the middle of silence
The stars descend in a heap
And I face the passing time,
Picking up the last star.

어떤 풍경화

벼랑에 햇살이 날려 쌓이는 말은
어쩌면 남겨둔 눈빛일 거다.

시선이 닿는 곳마다
하늘거리는 모든 것이 영롱해진다.

저녁 늦은 시간에
세월을 가늠해 보지만
우리는 모두가 잠깐
머물다 가는 풍경으로 남는다.

아침 고운 이슬로
자리를 만들어 누웠다가
하루는 열리고
거기 사람의 이야기는
다시금 비롯되겠지.

Some landscape painting

The word that stacks by blowing of sunshine on the cliff
Might be eyeshine left behind.

Wherever glances are reached,
All the wavering things become bright and translucent.

Late in the evening,
Guessing the years but
We all remain a landscape
Which had stayed for a short time, then passed.

With the pretty morning dew
Making the place and laying down
One day opens and
The people's story of there
May start again.

이순 앞에서

요즘엔 손발이 자주 저려
한밤중에 깨어나 앉는다.

어둠은 창 밖에 가득하고
나는 누군가의 이름을 뇌인다.

이 깊은 밤에
문득 스치는 바람을 붙잡아
혼자만의 말을 건넨다.

아침은 어디만큼
다가오고 있을까.

세월은 삭히는 게 아니라
내가 녹아드는 것이리라.

Before the age of sixty

My hands and feet are often numb these days
So, I sit up after waking in the middle of the night.

The darkness is full outside the window
I repeat somebody's name.

In this deep night
With a sudden catch of the wind
I talk to myself.

Whereabouts is the morning
Coming?

The years are not soothed,
But I might be melted in it.

아무렇지도 않게 꽃은 피어나

안개가 걷혀 가는 산 끝자락에
밤새 산사의 풍경소리에 젖었던 바람이
설깬 잠결로
쏟아지는 햇살에 눈이 부시다.

젊은 날의 비망록이 탈색되어
다시 하얀 백지로 나타나
날아가 버린 나의 마음을 그리라 한다.

삶의 굽이굽이에
멍에로 따라와 생명을 잉태하게 한다.

제 힘으로도 어찌할 수 없는
사는 모습의 무게에 눌린다.

Flowers bloom indifferently

The end part of the mountain where the mist is being cleared
The wind, which was wet all night by the scenery's sound of the mountain temple
With a half-sober sleep,
Is dazzling by pouring sunshine.

The memorandum book of youth has been decolored and
Appeared again as a white paper,
Tells me to draw my blown heart.

In every ins and outs of life
It follows me as a yoke and makes me conceive life.

Incapable of my strength,
I am pressed by the weight of the way of living.

마음 어디에 · 1

내 마음에도
가을이 베이면

마음 가득 담긴 색소
단풍이겠지.

Somewhere in my mind · 1

In my mind also
If the autumn is permeated

Fully filled pigments in my mind,
It might be autumn foliage.

마음 어디에 · 2

호수 속 노을을
한 잔 마시고 싶다던 너
내가 노을에게 귀엣말로 일렀지.

공허한 마음
아파해 준 너
노을도 너와 같이 취하고 싶대.

Somewhere in my mind · 2

The sunset on the lake

You said you wanted to drink a cup of it

I told it to the sunset through a whisper.

The hollow mind

You've been sick together

The sunset said that it also wanted to get drunk with you.

마음 어디에 · 3

차창 밖 코스모스 같은 손길이
이산가족의 뒷모습이다.

상봉 후 유품은
고뇌와 허무 뿐.

찻길 따라오는 구름이야
세월이 얼마나 그리웠으랴.

Somewhere in my mind · 3

The touch like cosmos flower outside a car window,
It's the back view of a separated family.

Keepsakes after the reunion
Are just anguish and futility.

The cloud that follows the road,
How much did it miss the years?

모습 그 여운으로

눈발이 날리는 골목길 보안등 불빛 아래
웅크린 그림자와 함께 마중 나왔지.

좋지 않은 시력으로
애써 나를 알아보고
'밤이 참 어두워요. 추운데 뭘 나왔어요'
비좁은 골목길이
외로움을 더해주는 그리움이었지.

손끝에 닿는 시린 체감 속
황홀한 정취라면
서로 주인으로서
실망도 후회도 모르게
나는 너에게 사로잡히고
너는 나에게 동화되었지.

A shape, with that lingering imagery

Under the security light in the alley where the snowflakes are blowing,
Came out to meet you with a crouched shadow.

With a poor eyesight
Noticing me with efforts and
"It's very dark. You should have stayed at home."
A narrow alleyway was
The longing that added the loneliness.

The inside of chilly feeling at the end of fingers,
If it were bewitched mood,
As an owner of each other
Without knowing neither disappointment nor regret
I am captivated by you and
You have been assimilated to me.

그리움은 얼굴을 맞대고 보는 것이 아니라
모습, 그 여운으로 피어나는 것이었지.
희미하게 보이는 불빛향기보다
그 어떤 고통도 오래하진 않으리.

우리가 지금
다만 흐르고 있구나 싶어.

The longing was not about looking face to face,
But to bloom as a shape, with that lingering imagery.
Than the fragrance of faint lights,
No certain anguish would last long.

I feel like we are
Now just flowing.

비어 있는 음향

안개 속으로
손에 잡힐 듯 다가온 마중의 그림자.

목탁 소리가 미명을 다듬어
보이지 않아도 볼 수 있는 소리
살아있는 것의 슬픔이다.

이승에서 저승까지 넘나드는 소리
육신을 일그러지게 하는 무서움이다.
되돌아보면 몸부림쳐 사는 것.
가랑잎이 하늘에 닿지 않는 손짓으로
죽지 못해 사는 이들의
저마다의 꿈을 울린다.

Empty sound

Into the fog
Almost touching the shadow of a welcoming, which comes closer.

So, the sound of the moktak trims the daybreak
Even invisible, but visible sound,
It's the sorrow of being alive.

The sound which transfers in and out from this life to the afterlife,
It's a fear that crumples the body.
If looking back, it's struggling to live a life.
The dead leaves with the unreachable gesture of hand to the sky
Resonate each one's dream of
The living person due to the impossibility of death.

산다는 것에 대한 정체 모를 이치
하나는 흔들리고 다른 하나는 시들어가도
목숨 하나하나 지탱해주는 힘이 어디 없겠는가.
하늘 한 구석
가두어 두었던 숨결
버려도 버림이 아니었다.

본래 목탁소리는 비어 있는 음향인가
무엇을 찾고 있다면
너의 흔들리는 길을 거기 잡아두고
발길을 더 어둠으로 돌리라.

The unknown logic of living

Even if one is swaying and the other is withered,

Where couldn't there be the power to support each life?

A corner of the sky

The breath of being trapped,

It was not abandoned even if it was thrown away.

Is the original voice of moktak Empty sound?

What if you are looking for something,

Hold your shaking path there, then

Turn your feet further into darkness.

설해목

마음에 묻어둔 말일지라도
가끔씩 헛기침으로나
하늘 자락 흔드는 소나무.

당신은 도대체 어떤 깨달음으로
눈 덮인 산의 말을 듣는가.

시간이 가면 갈수록
또렷한 그리움이
찬란한 빛깔로 떠오른다.

제 무게를 이기지 못한
설해목.

거긴 아무 말이 없고
그저 자취만 남았을 뿐이다.

The broken tree by heavy snow

Although it's buried word in its mind,
Sometimes even as a dry cough
The pine tree shakes the edge of the sky.

With what kind of enlightenment do you
Listen to the world of the mountain covered in snow?

As time goes by
The clear longing is
Rising as splendid colors.

Failing to sustain its own weight,
The broken tree by heavy snow.

There's nothing to say,
But only traces remain.

꽃씨

서랍 속 자유 하나
다른 풍습과 종교라도
땅 속 깊이 묻어두고
무엇인가 기다렸어야지.

꽃씨의
설렘을 누가 알랴.

불타올랐을 관능이여
겹눈질로 바라본 역광의 빛에
그래도 비탈로 서 있지 않았는가.
어찌 작은 모습일지라도 옳은 것에 있으리라,
그 속에 순수를 먹고 그와의 감성으로 살리라.

지순함으로
못 잊은 일을 삭히기엔 서럽잖았나.

A flower seed

One freedom in the drawer
No matter what it had another custom and religion
Buried it deep in the ground,
Should have waited for something.

Who would know
The tremble of the flower seed?

The sensuality that must have burned,
In the backlight which had been seen by a compound eye
Didn't it still stand on the slope?
Even if it might be small, but would exist in the right thing,
Would eat purity in it and live as sensibility with it.

With utmost innocence
Wasn't it sad to soothe things you haven't forgotten?

진실밖에 모르던 시절
꽃도 구름도
자기 모습만은 그릴 줄 몰랐다.

주소 불명으로 되돌아 온 편지 봉투에
쓸쓸한 가을 한 자락
싸둔 꽃씨가 자기 숨소리를 듣는다.
숨소리가 푸름을 가꾸고
푸름의 눈빛으로
얼마나 스스로 다스렸는가.

마음 가득 차 있는 진실
그 시절의 지금은
무슨 이유로 나를 떠나지 않는가.

The days when the truth was all
Neither flowers nor clouds,
They didn't know how to draw their own shape.

The envelop that is returned with an unknown address
One part of lonely autumn
The wrapped flower seed hears its own breath sound.
The breath sound decorates its blue
With that blue eyes
How much did it control itself?

The truth that fills the mind
The present time at those days
Wherefore didn't it leave me?

봄은 정녕 자네의 눈빛일세

세상이야 속절없다 하더라도
어디 아쉬움 하나 남겨 놓고 가는가 말일세.
겨울 지나면 어김없이 오는 봄 향기
자네 기운차게 해 주지 않던가 말일세.
헛고생을 시켜도 그 만큼 행복일 걸세.
행복이 지나쳐 심심해지면
심심한 것끼리 세상을 사랑하게 놔두면 되느니
그 세상은 항상 봄이 될 걸세.
몇 날을 두고 과거같이 손길이 닿지 않아
피가 흐르는 육신이 여위어만 가도
그래, 봄은 정녕 자네의 포근한 눈빛일세.

The spring is truly your eyes

The world is helpless though,
It really doesn't leave anything of regrets.
After winter, the spring's fragrance is surely coming
Maybe, it really makes you invigorate.
Even though it makes you do useless efforts, as much as that, you will be happy.
If happiness is excessive, then gets bored,
Just let those boring things love the world, among themselves
That world would be always spring.
The touch of hand hasn't reached like past for several days,
Even if the body with flowing its blood goes thin,
Yes, spring is truly your warm eyes.

한 그루 나무로 서서

아름다움을 담기 위한 그릇일레.
말을 적게 하면서
침묵을 헤아릴 줄 아는 사람으로
아름다운 사귐과 대화이어라.
한 골 물이 되었으니
모난 돌 굴러 둥글게 다듬어 가꾸고 다스려라.
행복은 욕심과 고집을 하나씩 버리고
구름바람이 하늘에 닿도록
지켜주는 연민이어라.
줄 것도 바랄 것도 없을 때까지
무엇을 버리고 채우려는가 속다짐하다가
속마음을 꽃으로 피어내어라.
순수 앞에서 말없는 표정으로
속마음 읽어내는 사랑이어라.
속된 말에도 허리를 낮추고
한 그루 나무를 닮아가며
바람 한 점 잠재울 줄 알아라.
제자리를 지키는 기다림의 사랑이어라.
서로가 눈빛 하나라도
만져서 손때 묻은 정이라 하라.

Standing as a tree

Will be a bowl for filling beauty.
While speaking less
As a person who can fathom silence,
Hope to be a beautiful acquaintance and conversation.
Because of becoming water in one valley,
Roll the angular stones and round them up and govern them.
Happiness is that throwing away greed and persistence one by one and
So that the cloud wind reaches the sky,
Hope to be the compassion for guarding it.
Until then there's nothing to give and desire,
Determining what to clear and to fill,
Hope to bloom that inner mind like a flower.
With a silent look in front of purity,
Hope to be the love that can read the inner mind.
Lowering my waist even in vulgar word and
Resembling a tree,
Know to calm down one part of the winds.
Hope to be the love of waiting to keep its own place.
Even one eye glance at each other,
Call it the affection stained with traces of hands.

鄭松田 시인

- 1962년 「시와 시론」으로 등단.
- 서라벌예술대학 문예창작과 졸.
- 중앙대학교 국문과 및 동 대학원 졸.
- 용인시 죽전중학교 교장, 한라대학교,
  경기대학교 겸임교수 역임.
- 세계시문학회 회장 역임.
- 한국자유시인협회 본상, 세계시문학상 대상,
  경기도문학상 대상, 경기예술 대상, 현대 시인상 수상.
- 한국현대시인협회 지도위원, 한국작가협회 최고위원.
- 한국현대시인협회, 세계시문학회, 미당 시맥회 회원.

■ 시집

「그리움의 무게」,「바람의 침묵」,「꽃과 바람」,
「빛의 울림을 그린다」,「내 이렇게 살다가」,「바람의 말」.

■ 자작시 감상 선집

「그리움과 사랑의 되풀이」,「자연과 우주의 너울」,
「내 삶의 소용돌이」,「내 인생의 뒤안길」.

■ 한영시집

「숨은 꽃」,「너를 맞아 보낸다」,「꽃과 아내」,
「너와의 걸음걸이」

Poet Song-jun Jung

- Debuted with 「Poems and Poetics」 in 1962
- Graduated Literary Creation from Seorabeol University of Arts
- Received and graduated master's degree from Joong-ang University
- School president of Jukjeon Middle School in Yong-in City. Served as affiliated professor of Hanla University and Kyeongki University
- Served as the president of Literary Society of the World Poetry
- Awardee of Korea Free Poet Association, first line up at World Poetry Literature Award, first line up at Kyeonggido Literature Award, first line up at Kyeonggi Art Award, the receipient of the Modern Poet Award.
- Direction committee of Korea Modern Poet Association, the executive committee of Korea Author Association
- Member of Korea Modern Poset Association, World Poet Literary Society, and Midang Poet Line Association

■ Collections of Poems

「The weight of longing」, 「The silence of the wind」, 「Flower and wind」, 「Drawing the echo of lights」, 「Iliving in such way」, 「The words of the wind」.

■ Collection of poems for appreciation

「Repetition of longing and love」, 「The swell of nature and universe」, 「Whirlpool of my life」, 「Backwaters of my life」.

■ Korean-English Poems

「The hidden flower」, 「Sending you after meeting you」, 「Flowers and my wife」, 「Walking with you」

정송전 한영시집 4
너와의 걸음걸이

2022년 8월 18일 1판 1쇄 인쇄
2022년 8월 22일 1판 1쇄 발행

지은이 | 정송전
펴낸이 | 김효열

펴낸곳 | **을지출판공사**

등록번호 | 1985년 2월 14일 제2-741호
주　　소 | 서울시 마포구 양화진길 41, 603호
우편번호 | 04083
대표전화 | 02) 334-4050
팩시밀리 | 02) 334-4010
전자우편 | ejp4050@hanmail.net

값 12,000원

ISBN 978-89-7566-217-1　　　03810

Korean-English Poems Collection of Jeong Song Jeon 4
Walking with you

1st edition printed August 18, 2022
1st edition published August 22, 2022

Author   Jeong Song Jeon
Publisher Kim Hyo Yeol

Published EulJi Publishing Company

Registration 1985. 2. 14 No. 2-741
Address 603. 41, Yanghwajin-gil, Mapo-go, Seoul, Korea
Phone 02-334-4050   Fax 02-334-4010
e-mail ejp4050@hanmail.net

Value 12,000 won

ISBN 978-89-7566-217-1   03810